YOUR KNOWLEDGE HAS VALUE

- We will publish your bachelor's and master's thesis, essays and papers

- Your own eBook and book - sold worldwide in all relevant shops

- Earn money with each sale

Upload your text at www.GRIN.com
and publish for free

Bibliographic information published by the German National Library:

The German National Library lists this publication in the National Bibliography; detailed bibliographic data are available on the Internet at http://dnb.dnb.de .

This book is copyright material and must not be copied, reproduced, transferred, distributed, leased, licensed or publicly performed or used in any way except as specifically permitted in writing by the publishers, as allowed under the terms and conditions under which it was purchased or as strictly permitted by applicable copyright law. Any unauthorized distribution or use of this text may be a direct infringement of the author s and publisher s rights and those responsible may be liable in law accordingly.

Imprint:

Copyright © 2016 GRIN Verlag, Open Publishing GmbH
Print and binding: Books on Demand GmbH, Norderstedt Germany
ISBN: 9783668242715

This book at GRIN:

http://www.grin.com/en/e-book/334153/sleeping-with-the-enemy-1991-martin-burney-as-an-example-of-obsessive

William Bell

"Sleeping with the Enemy" (1991). Martin Burney as an example of Obsessive Compulsive Personality Disorder?

Analysis with the Diagnostic and Statistical Manual of Mental Disorders (DSM-5)

GRIN - Your knowledge has value

Since its foundation in 1998, GRIN has specialized in publishing academic texts by students, college teachers and other academics as e-book and printed book. The website www.grin.com is an ideal platform for presenting term papers, final papers, scientific essays, dissertations and specialist books.

Visit us on the internet:

http://www.grin.com/

http://www.facebook.com/grincom

http://www.twitter.com/grin_com

Table of Contents

Introduction 2
DSM Criterion 2
Examples of OCPD 2
Categorical Information 4
Borderline Personality Disorder Traits 6
Narcissistic Personality Disorder Traits 7
Schizophrenia Trait 8
Dimensional Information 8
Medical Problem(s) 8
Psychosocial Problems 8
Examples of Narcissistic Personality Disorder 9
Examples of Borderline Personality Disorder 11

Introduction

Movie watched: *Sleeping with the Enemy* (Joseph Ruben, 1991, 20th Century Fox).

Character observed: Martin Burney, a married, white male in his late twenties-early thirties.

Diagnosis: Obsessive-compulsive personality disorder (OCPD).

DSM Criterion

According to the Diagnostic and Statistical Manual of Mental Disorder (5th ed.; DSM-5; American Psychiatric Association [APA], 2013);. Obsessive Compulsive Personality Disorder (OCPD) is indicated when four (or more) criteria are met (APA, 2013). Martin Burney meets four of the criteria for OCPD.

All examples of OCPD diagnostic behavior by Martin Birney appear in the 1993 film *Sleeping With the Enemy (*producer, director, year of release).

Examples of OCPD

1. "Is preoccupied with details, rules, lists, order, organization, or schedules to the extent that the major point of the activity is lost" (APA, 2013).

    Specific examples-

    Martin seductively embraces Laura; she thinks he wants more sex. He then orders her to "come with me" and leads her (by the hand, trailing behind him) to the bathroom where he forces her to determine what (in his opinion) is wrong. Laura quickly glances around and spots that the bathroom towels are not aligned perfectly, she quickly fixes them.

    Laura frantically line-up groceries in kitchen cupboard, it is obvious to viewer that she fears Martin's retribution should he find them not to his satisfaction.

    As Martin and Laura have intercourse, we see his shoes lined-up perfectly near bed, socks rolled perfectly and centered between shoes, Martin's clothes are folded perfectly and draped, perfectly centered over the back of chair near bed, Martin's belt is hung (exactly in the middle) over his slacks .

After he climaxes, Martin immediately heads for the shower.

Laura asks Martin if his dinner has ever been late, even once. (Martin obviously has insisted his dinner be made exactly on time every night they eat at home).

3. "Is excessively devoted to work and productivity to the exclusion of leisure activities and friendships…" (APA, 2013).

Specific examples-

Martin approaches wife on beach, walks across expanse of sand at their vacation home dressed in full business suit, complete with overcoat.

Martin admits to his wife, Laura that he is working while they are on their vacation.

4. "Is overconscientious, scrupulous, and inflexible about matters of morality, ethics, and values…" (APA, 2013).

Specific examples-

Upon admitting on the beach that he is working on their vacation, Martin overcompensates and attempts to sound as if he cares about Laura's opinion as he asks her, "do you forgive me?"

After Laura smudges small amount of sand on him Martin says he will change clothes.

At party, Laura asks Martin, "Have I been social long enough?" Laura has subordinated herself to the rigorous demands of Martin.

After Martin has beaten Laura, says to her, "Now you'll pout and spoil our supper."

Martin tells Laura to conquer her fears (of water).

Martin has slugged Laura and kicked her afterwards as she lay on the floor. Once he leaves the room. Laura immediately begins picking up the flowers that have fallen to the floor lest she incur Martin's additional wrath for allowing a mess to lie on floor.

Martin reminds Laura that his dinner was late when Laura went away (ostensibly) to her mother's funeral.

Martin pats mouth with a kerchief after drinking water from a water fountain.

8. "Shows rigidity and stubbornness" (APA, 2013).

Specific examples-

Martin passive-aggressively tells Laura that he wants her to wear a black dress to the party instead of the white one she has chosen, even though she is already wearing the white dress.

As Martin speaks to doctor at dock near sailboat, he tells doctor that he tries to get Laura out on a boat, "at least once a season," after he has told doctor that she nearly drowned as a kid, hates the water, and cannot swim.

Martin calls the doctor Laura's "friend" even though Laura has said she does not know doctor. Martin implies he and Laura will be sailing that evening, and that she must not protest.

Martin tells Laura that the discussion they are having about her working more days at the library is postponed until after they go sailing.

Categorical Information

Martin's preoccupation with rules, order, organization and schedules (APA, 2013) interferes with the enjoyment of his marriage to Laura: He brings Laura inside the house to force Laura to rearrange bathroom towels. Laura then hurries to kitchen and hurriedly arranges groceries perfectly in kitchen cabinet. Martin arranges clothes too carefully before he and Laura have sex, and after he climaxes, he immediately runs to the shower. Martin is "excessively devoted to work …to the exclusion of leisure activities and friendships…" (APA, 2013): Martin is going into the office in full business attire while he and Laura are on vacation at beach house, leaving Laura at home alone. Even upon returning from work, Martin walks to the beach in his business suit indicating that the fun is over, he has not put on shorts and come to join his wife in the fun of digging for clams.

Martin is "over-conscientious, scrupulous, and inflexible about matter of morality, ethics, or values…" (APA, 2013). From the way his wife, Laura, cleans up messes, Martin appears to insist the house is spotless and that every item must be in a very specific place-the bathroom towels, his clothes hung perfectly over a chair before he has sex, changing suit after small amount of sand gets on it. Martin's inflexibility about morality, ethics, or values is apparent when he insists the Laura go sailing with him even though she hates the water.

Martin "shows rigidity and stubbornness" (APA, 2013) when he passive-aggressively tells Laura that he does not like the dress she has already chosen for that evening's party and tells her to wear a different dress, instead. Even though Laura has said she does not know the doctor, Martin calls the doctor Laura's friend. At the boat dock, Martin tells the doctor that he likes to get Laura out on the water in a boat at least once a year even though she hates water and does not swim. Martin will not resolve his discussion with Laura about her working more days at library. Instead, he says the discussion is "postponed" until after they go sailing.

Although Martin exhibits enough categorical symptoms to warrant a primary diagnosis of OCPD, an OCPD diagnosis does not account for Martin's fear of abandonment, rage, selfishness, egotistical behavior, and his violence. Those traits warrant an (undiagnosed) mention as secondary personality disorders containing the symptoms of borderline personality disorder, narcissistic personality disorder, and schizophrenia..

Borderline Personality Disorder Traits

According to the DSM 5, Martin exhibits "frantic efforts to avoid real or imagined abandonment." (APA,2013) when he accuses Laura of having an affair with the doctor, when he beat Laura after she returned from her mother's "funeral", when he told her right after their honeymoon that if she ever left him, he would track her down and find her anywhere. Upon realizing that Laura has left him, Martin begins a systematic campaign to find Laura.

Martin also exhibits the borderline personality characteristic of 'inappropriate, intense anger or difficulty controlling anger (frequent display of temper...physical fights (APA, 2013). Martin slugs Laura to the ground and then kicks her. When Martin thinks he has lost Laura at sea, he throws the wedding gift he gave her through the living room window. After leaving Martin, Laura tells the woman on the bus that Martin has been beating her for the past three and a half years, since right after their honeymoon. Martin wields a gun against a stranger and threatens him with death if stranger goes to police. At end of film, Martin beats Laura's boyfriend and nearly kills him, and then attempts to murder Laura.

Martin's behavior of being nice to Laura one moment, angry the next, and then nice again, when he admires her hard work with the clam-digging, then beats her in a jealous rage only to then tell her he's sorry, calls her "princess," and then goes out and buys her a dress, meets the borderline personality criteria of "extremes of idealization and devaluation" (APA,2013).

Martin also meets the borderline personality disorder diagnosis of "transient, stress-related paranoid ideation…" (APA, 2013). Martin imagines an affair between the doctor and Laura (and later accuses her of such) when Martin becomes stressed from the doctor's mention of seeing Laura in the window of the beach home. Finally, although Martin's arranging of the groceries in Laura's rented home would appear to be symptomatic of his OCPD, his incremental arranging of the towels in order to terrify Laura do not follow the pattern of a compulsion for order. If that were the case,

Martin would have fully lined-up all of the towels when he first saw them, as he would have been unable to otherwise. Instead, Martins actions represent a paranoid response to the abandonment of him by Laura.

Narcissistic Personality Disorder Traits

The "Associated Features Supporting Diagnosis" section of narcissistic personality disorder states that an individual exhibiting traits of this disorder may react with rage at being criticized (APA, 2013). After Laura reminds Martin of his beating of her upon her returning from her mother's funeral, Martin tells Laura that it seems to him that Laura is provoking an argument so that she will be "unable to sail tonight." Martin then postpones the discussion until, "After our sail," implying he will beat Laura after the sail.

Among the diagnostic criteria for narcissistic personality disorder that Martin fits are that having a 'grandiose sense of self-importance," (APA, 2013). Martin tells the doctor that he, too, is also a boater. Martin also believes that he is "special and unique and can only be understood by, or should associate with, other special or high-status people…" (APA, 2013). When Laura disappears off boat during a storm, Martin demands of Coast Guard that another boat and a helicopter be employed in the search. When Martin hires a detective to find Laura's mother, Martin tells detective, "I want this taken seriously" and offers a bonus to agency when they find Laura's mother and to the detective who finds her.

Martin also fits the DSM 5 narcissistic personality disorder diagnostic criteria of "requires excessive admiration" (APA, 2013). The morning after beating Laura and then forcing her to have sex with him, Martin sees Laura touching a sculpture in the living room and says to her, "Thinking of our honeymoon? The night I gave you that? The night I taught you to dance?" After Martin has tracked down Laura and broken into her house, and beaten her boyfriend, he grabs Laura, tries to initiate a dance with her, and says once more, "Remember our honeymoon, how I taught you to dance?"

Criterion 9 for narcissistic personality disorder stipulates that a person with this disorder will "show arrogant, haughty behaviors or attitudes" (APA, 2013). Martin devalues a close friendship with the Blanchards to Laura, characterizing the Blanchard's party, to which he and Laura are invited as "stupid." Also, after breaking into her rented house and forcing Laura to send away her boyfriend who is knocking on her door, Martin tells Laura, "He doesn't matter, he's nothing."

Schizophrenia Trait

List Main Diagnosis. Then consider does your client show any other symptoms of other disorders present but not the main diagnosis? Make sure to note here if you saw any symptoms of other disorders, even if it does not warrant a diagnosis. Discuss other symptoms and illustrate those symptoms with examples.

Dimensional Information

Make sure to assign a number here. Make sure to explain at what point in the movie you are giving the number and why you chose that particular number.

Medical Problem(s)

Any medical concerns, if not, still address, but just say you did not observe any.

Psychosocial Problems

Must address this with examples from the film. Make sure to include examples from your client (in the movie) of the environmental stressors they experienced. All of the movies have lots of these! That is what the plot of the movie is Narcissistic Personality Disorder, Borderline Personality Disorder, Narcissistic Personality Disorder is indicated when five (or more) criteria are met (APA, 2013). Martin Birney meets five criteria for Narcissistic Personality. Borderline Personality Disorder is indicated when five (or more) criteria are met (APA, 2013). Martin Birney meets five criteria for Borderline Personality Disorder

Examples of Narcissistic Personality Disorder

1. "Has a grandiose sense of self-importance (e.g. exaggerates achievements and talents, expect to be recognized as superior without commensurate achievements)" (APA, 2013).

    4:49: Martin looks across yard while he and Laura are at a party, he keeps staring at her until her eyes meet his.

    16:25: After beating her, Martin has selfish sex with Laura, he is not shown helping her achieve orgasm and viewer does not see Laura have an orgasm, after he climaxes, he does not cuddle or engage in 'after-play", he immediately leaves room and goes to shower (see OCPD).

2. "Is preoccupied with fantasies of unlimited success, power, brilliance, beauty, or ideal love" (APA,2013).

    19:24: "Requires excessive admiration" (APA, 2013).

    9:11: When Martin goes to dock to speak with the doctor on the sailboat, he remains standing on the higher platform above as he speaks so that the doctor will be looking up to him.

    9:15: Martin proceeds to tell doctor how he is also a sailor.

    16:28; After his one-sided intercourse session with Laura during which it is obvious she cannot stand him, she forces herself to smile at Martin so he will believe she liked the sex.

3. "Has a sense of entitlement (i.e. unreasonable expectation of especially favorable treatment or automatic compliance with his or her expectations" (APA, 2013).

After they arrive home from the party, Laura wants to make sure Martin is satisfied in every way, so she asks if he is hungry and he tells her he is. As Laura begins to make a snack in the kitchen, Martin suddenly grabs Laura and knocks the food she is holding to the floor. Laura's serving Martin's desires has aroused him and he now wants to have sex with her, so, even if Laura is hungry, she must prioritize Martin's needs first.

10:50: After beating and kicking Laura, Martin tells her, "now you'll pout." Next he says to her, "I'm so sorry, won't you smile?"

11:53; Tells Laura to go sailing. Says to her, "Do it. For me."

14:45; Martin mischaracterizes his earlier beating of Laura, discounts his part in starting and escalating it, and creates a part for Laura in her own beating by saying, "I'm sorry we quarreled."

23:59: After Laura has fallen into the sea, Martin tells the coast guard, "We've got have another boat and a helicopter, get back on the radio, please."

54:25: Martin tells private detective, "I want this taken very seriously."

4. "Lacks empathy: is unwilling to recognize or identify with the feelings and needs of others" (APA, 2013).

10:56: As Laura lays crying on floor after Martin has hit and kicked her, he yells "stop it" at her.

12:15: After beating Laura, Martin dismisses whole incident as if it never happened, says he's going into town.

17:21: As Laura serves Martin on the patio and sits down at table with him, Martin says, "You want something, I know my Princess."

17:34: Laura tells Martin that "the library" has offered her a full time position. He answers, "You already work three days a week and I support that ."

17:38: Laura tells Martin she wants to work more, he asks her, "What about out home, don't you love our home as much?"

Examples of Borderline Personality Disorder

1. "Frantic efforts to avoid real or imagined abandonment…" (APA, 2013).

    4:34: As they enter party, Martin keeps a grip on Laura as he guides her through the front year, into the house, and finally they come to a stop at a group of people.

    11:41: After accusing Laura of having an affair with the doctor and beating her and telling her that he is forcing her to go on a boat which he believes she hates and fears, Martin calls Laura "princess" and says he'll "be right there, right by your side."

    31:09: Laura tells woman on bus that Martin told her early in their relationship that if Laura ever left him, he would find her and punish her, adding that he would never let her go, and that he would find her anywhere.

    45:27: When Martin realizes that Laura is still alive, he begins a frantic search through her things looking for clues as to her whereabouts and makes a huge (uncharacteristic) mess in the house.

    46:50: When Martin finds Laura's wedding ring in the toilet, he puts it on his finger even though he knows that she has not died, but that she has left him.

    50:00: Martin begins a quest to stalk and find Laura by first going to the last rest home that he knew Laura's mother lived.

    54:25: Martin tells private eye that he is will pay a ten thousand dollar bonus to the detective who finds Laura's mother.

2. "A pattern of unstable and intense interpersonal relationships characterized by extremes of idealization and devaluation" (APA, 2013).

2:46: 3:05; Martin tells Laura, "I missed you" and kisses her. He will beat, kick, and practically rape her the next evening.

3. Affective instability due to a marked reactivity of mood (e.g. intense episodic dysphoria, irritability, or anxiety usually lasting a few hours and only rarely more than a few days)" (APA, 2013).

2:46: Martin good mood.because Laura is catering to his needs.

10:29: Martin, real bad mood, irrationally thinks Laura having an affair with doctor.

11:20: Martin good mood; after beating Laura, Martin has control again

18:16: Martin bad mood, tells Laura that she snuck off to go to her mother's "funeral".

18:45: Martin real bad mood, Implies to Laura, that if she keeps talking about her mother's funeral and wanting to work more, she will be so severely beaten that she will be unable to sailing that evening.

4. Inappropriate, intense anger or difficulty controlling anger (e.g. frequent displays of temper, constant anger, recurrent physical fights)" (APA, 2013).

5. 19:03: When Martin postpones the conversation about Laura working more, a beating later is implied.

25:07: When Martin returns home after Laura is presumably lost at sea, He heaves the heavy honeymoon gift statue that he bought for Laura through the large plate glass living room window of the beach house. He feels has been abandoned.

30:39: Laura tells sympathetic female passenger on bus that Martin started beating her right after their honeymoon, three and a half years earlier..

6. Transient, stress-related paranoid ideation or severe dissociative symptoms"(APA, 2013).

10:29: Martin accuses Laura of having doctor in the house while Martin was away.

10:35: When Laura denies knowing doctor, Martin tells her, "sure you do" then, he hits Laura hard in the face, and yells at her, "Does it give you that much pleasure to humiliate me?

44:55: Once Martin hears woman from YWCA describe Laura swimming, he realizes that Laura is alive and has left him, and that the woman on the phone has seen Laura's injuries

YOUR KNOWLEDGE HAS VALUE

- We will publish your bachelor's and master's thesis, essays and papers

- Your own eBook and book - sold worldwide in all relevant shops

- Earn money with each sale

Upload your text at www.GRIN.com
and publish for free